LEADING WHILE BROKEN

DR. DEMETRA M. WILLIAMS

To leaders everywhere.
May you find the strength
and the courage to lead others as
you piece together the broken parts of you.

CONTENTS

ACKNOWLEDGMENTS

To my Savior- the Lord of my life- Jesus Christ – I still don't know what I did to deserve your grace, mercy and blessings. Thank you for choosing me!

To my husband/pastor, Jeffery – Thank you for loving me through all of this. You didn't give up on me and I am grateful. I still say, "I do." I love you, always and forever.

To my son, Jeffery "Trey" – You are amazing, and I can't wait to see what God has in store for you. Mommy loves you!

To my family – the Gastons, Williamses, Facens, Powells, Brookses, Lawsons and Walkers – Your love has lifted me for many years, and I love and appreciate you all.

To my best friends, sister girls, my sorors and MY SQUAD – what's understood doesn't have to be said.

PREFACE

The end of a matter is better than its beginning, and
patience is better than pride
(Eccles. 7:8 NIV)

We lie to ourselves. We lie to others. It happens all
the time.

How or when, you ask? When someone asks, "H*ow*
are you doing?" We are so accustomed to saying that
we are fine that we utter it without thought. If most
of us take the time to think about how we truly feel
when people greet us with those four words, the
majority of people could attest to the fact that we
are **<u>not</u>** okay.

In fact, at this very moment- while reading this book- you're probably going through something that you have never shared with another person. For some, what you're facing is small... for others, what you're facing has shattered you; Don't look at the devastating situations as hindrances, they are benefits in the long run.

It always amazes me how our greatest blessings can sometimes come from our greatest adversities. The very thing that we thought would make us throw in the towel sometimes propels us to our next level. The test, the trial, the storm-the one that was meant to take you out- only strengthens you.

Leaders everywhere want people to believe that everything is okay. Many put on a grand façade, but on the inside, they are picking up the pieces. Some have mastered "the look," a guise of smiles and laughs cloaking pain and anguish, duping others into think that they have it all together.

The problem is that an overwhelming majority of leaders have **no one** to talk to about their issues, their hurts, and their problems. They don't have safe places where they can confess and unpack the levels of their brokenness. Many leaders rarely have the opportunity to put their leadership role down and solely focus on themselves.

For this reason, there are many bishops, pastors, teachers, evangelists, COOs, CEOs, presidents, executives, husbands, wives and parents in leadership roles- *leading while broken.*

My personal experience and triumph over a season of brokenness inspired me to share with you what God has shared with me. In this book, I will be transparent about how God graced me to lead and navigate my brokenness simultaneously.

I pray that as you read, God will reveal himself to you as plainly as he did to me. I pray that he heals your brokenness and gives you the strength needed to lead. You are not alone.

FOREWORD

Dear Reader,

You're in for a rewarding and encouraging experience as you turn the pages of this book, as have I, with every encounter I've had with Dr. DeMetra Williams.

Dr. Williams is authentic, smart, driven, determined and selfless. Her beauty is an added incentive to an exhaustive list of qualities housed within her. She is a trendsetter and one to emulate as it relates to being a wife, mother and educator! Dr. DeMetra Williams has always been a beautiful soul with a cheerful and winning personality.

People everywhere are multi-talented and faceted; however, that does not exempt anyone from hurt, let down and disappointment! Regardless of your title, position or status in society or in the church- I'm certain you will have a unique encounter as you read *Leading While Broken*.

There's not a person on the face of the earth who hasn't been broken or felt broken in some way. Many times, we try to mask it (or we're ashamed of it), but eventually, it comes out one way or another!

Dr. Williams will be quite the guide on this journey of self-reflection and assessment. Her transparency and authenticity will bring healing, wholeness and deliverance to leaders everywhere fighting a silent battle with brokenness.

Psalms 34:18 states, *The Lord is nigh unto them that are of a broken heart; and saveth such as be of a contrite spirit.* With the help of God and the steps outlined in this book, every reader will be better equipped to serve as leaders in wholeness and with confidence.

Lady Stephanie Dillard

First Lady, Citadel Church of God in Christ

First Lady, Tennessee Metro Jurisdiction

First Lady, COGIC International AIM Convention

RECOGNIZING BROKENNESS WITHIN

*Take heed that ye do not your alms before men, to be
seen of them:
otherwise ye have no reward of your Father which is
in heaven
(Matthew 6:1)*

"Y ou better recognize," was a saying that we
used growing up. It meant that whoever
we were talking to needed to realize and
understand who we *really* were and that we
meant *business*.

Likewise, it is vital to recognize when you are
broken. Brokenness is not always easy to recognize or
identify. Sometimes, if you have been broken for an

extended period of time, being broken seems *normal*.

You may be wondering; how can I tell if I am broken? Below is a list that can assist you with conducting a self-assessment. **Not all** of these will apply to you; however, if you identify with any of these situations, it highly possible that you may be in a broken state right now.

· You find yourself wanting to be alone more.

· At your job/ministry, you find yourself going through the motions.

· You find yourself not praying like you used to.

· You find it hard to sleep at night because you are thinking of everything that has gone wrong throughout the day (or even throughout your life).

· You can't seem to find time to pick up the Bible.

· You seem a bit more pessimistic about life. You remember a time where you were more optimistic.

· You don't feel as close to God anymore. You detect a noticeable distance in your relationship with him.

· You are ready to give up. You are days away from quitting, or you have noticed a pattern of self-discouragement.

· You start to question if you even want to be "fixed." You find yourself able to live and operate in the broken space with ease.

· You feel guilty about things you have done, and you suppress your feelings because you feel like no one will understand.

· You feel like you are in a rut that you cannot seem to break free from.

· Your emotions are becoming more and more unreliable and unstable.

If you identify with more of these than you initially thought, don't fret! When you know better, you can do better, and that's what *Leading While Broken* is going to teach you.

In my case, I knew there was *something* wrong... but I didn't know *what*. I found myself going through the motions in my church, my job, and my marriage. Whether it was actually true or not, I felt like a complete failure in most of the aspects of my life.

At the time, it seemed like the only thing I was good at was being a mom. In fact, I intentionally poured more love into my son because I knew motherhood was the only thing that seemed to be going well in my life.

Yet, I wanted people to think I had it all together. I learned how to put on a mask. I perfected it so well that most people had no clue that I was going through anything. I had mastered the art of the disguise.

I'm certain many would say, "DeMetra lives the perfect life". After all, I have a good husband, a nice job, a nice house, a nice car, a good family and a good church. With all of that, I should have been happy, right? I wasn't. I was miserable. I felt like a stranger in a life that I could barely manage. I was in survival mode, and in order to protect my facade, I did *just enough* for people to think I was okay.

Being a leader, I felt pressured to function and complete my tasks successfully. I mastered being task-oriented; I busied and buried myself in work. I figured people only questioned things when productivity declined. I'd say to myself, *"Just keep working Dee, and no one will notice"*.

Most of all, I refused to look *weak*. That's a no, no for leaders- especially *women* in leadership. The thing is, I didn't *want* to be a leader at that time. Like many of you, I learned how to take my many hats on and off.

I acquired the art of being cordial while crying inside, of shaking hands while shaking fists internally... of smiling externally to suppress the screams within. I mastered leading while broken.

One day, I was sitting at my desk in the office- working on a church program. I heard a voice say, *"It's all in vain."* I looked around to see who was talking to me, but I didn't *see* anyone. I was shocked. Most of you would have been shocked at the voice; I was shocked because *I thought I was good.*

Revelation hit me like a sack of bricks. I had been operating in a broken stage for so long *it felt normal.* The voice returned, *"When will you recognize you are broken?"* I was still frozen at the realization that I had been functioning at half-capacity for God knows how long.

Once the realization hit me, I can honestly say, I did **not** know *what* to do. I was ashamed. Shame turned into disappointment as I reflected on the years I wasted going through the motions. I felt intense pain, frustration and desperation.

What hurt the most was that I didn't know how to *fix* it. Internally, I was picking myself apart. *How can you be a leader and* **not** *have a solution to your own problem? A leader should be able to fix problems.* For one of the first times in my life, I felt helpless. I had a serious problem that I couldn't fix.

Little did I know, that is exactly where God wanted me. He needed me in a mental space where I finally realized that it was out of my hands. He needed me to acknowledge the problem was much bigger than me, and to admit that I could **not** do it alone. He said, *"Everything you've gone through has been for My glory"*. Those words reassured me that it was time to place this brokenness in the hands that created and crafted me. Those words guaranteed I'd be fine.

So, I ask you this – if you're living in denial like I was, what will it take for you to realize and admit *you* are broken? If you've come to terms with it, what will you do now that you know?

No matter where you are in your self-assessment of brokenness, I'm here to help. The process to recovering from brokenness requires allowing God to work on you. Give God the broken pieces of your life; allow him to order your steps toward a journey of healing and restoration.

Prayer

Father God, I thank you for who you are and what you have done in my life. Thank you for allowing me to come to the realization that I am broken. I am hurting, and I don't know what to do. God, open my heart and my mind so I can be mended.

Give me a heart that is willing to let you in and a listening ear so I can hear what you say. Lord, I trust you in this process, and although I don't understand it fully, I submit to your sovereignty because doing things my way hasn't worked. I now understand that everything I've gone through has been for your glory and today, Lord, I give you all of me.

Reflect and Respond

It is important that we take time and reflect on what we've learned and evaluate ourselves in every step of this process as we journey through healing from brokenness.

*After every chapter, there will be a series of questions designed to thrust you into deep self-reflection and rumination on your life and your leadership style. Be sure to answer each question honestly. This is **your** journal.*

As leaders, we seldom discuss our pasts. We tend to pack memories from our childhood deep into the lattermost parts of our minds. This interactive journal is designed to bring all those memories and experiences to the forefront. The only way we can heal from brokenness is through unpacking and exposing the things that contributed to the cracks in our vessels. Trauma is one of those things.

Trauma isn't always easily recognizable. Sometimes we're affected by things as children that we don't think we carry into adulthood; things like everyday routines, our perceptions of strengths and weaknesses, and our beliefs, convictions and morals.

In Chapter 1, we discussed recognizing brokenness. Sometimes, we are unable to recognize brokenness because we brush over the traumas that contribute to it.

What are some traumas you've experienced, from childhood to now, that have affected you as a person and could be contributing factors to your feelings of brokenness? Identify each one and attempt to correlate which aspect of leadership each particular trauma most likely affects.

Take your time. Be detailed and specific.

_____

_____

_____

_____

_____

_____

_____

_____

_____

_____

_____

_____

_____

_____

_____

_____

_____

_____

_____

_____

_____

_____

_____

_____

_____

_____

_____

_____

_____

_____

_____

_____

_____

_____

_____

_____

_____

_____

DR. DEMETRA M. WILLIAMS

_____

_____

_____

_____

_____

_____

_____

_____

_____

_____

_____

_____

_____

_____

_____

_____

A BROKEN SURRENDER

Behold, as the clay is in the potter's hand,
so are ye in mine hand, O house of Israel.
(Jeremiah 18:6)

I f you are anything like me, you are probably trying to figure out what to do *now*. You may also find yourself in a vulnerable place. I consider myself a strong person, and I rarely allow myself to be put in compromising situations.

Vulnerability can be scary. I am always ready to help others get fixed. I love helping people and I am willing to pitch in whenever needed. **Working on me, however, was not as easy as working on others.** It was much harder than I expected.

As I stated in chapter one, leaders are problem solvers and action takers. People come to us with situations, and we often pride ourselves in being able to offer solutions to problems.

We think out of the box and get creative when it comes to dealing with everything and everyone else. Naturally, we should be able to fix ourselves... right?

Wrong.

I tried to fix myself and soon realized that *I was a part of my problem*! I attempted to mend and self-heal several times, only to discover that I was trying to put a Band-Aid on a gaping wound.

When that didn't work, I tried a self-imposed quarantine. I decided **not** to preach because I didn't want to share my hurt. When it came time for me to assign speakers, I choose others to speak. I figured if I 'sat myself down', *that* would be enough.

I didn't comprehend that I hadn't cleaned my wound properly and the resources I had to provide self-care were limited and inadequate. They just weren't enough. I needed hands that were bigger than mine; hands that had a more significant reach.

Most leaders are accustomed to being in control. It takes a peculiar person to be able to surrender their lives to someone else. Ironically, for some leaders, it takes hitting rock bottom before we can truly surrender any part of ourselves.

Although I did not hit rock bottom, I came painstakingly close. I was at a tough place in my life. I did everything in my power to pick myself up only to find that my strength was **not** enough. I could **not** do it on my own.

It came to the point that I understood I needed help, and I was finally willing to seek it. I was in over my head; this self-repair was above my pay grade. **Jesus paid the price, the ultimate sacrifice, and because that price was paid, I could go to *God*.**

Amid the hurt, pain, shame and guilt, I was relieved knowing I could go to God. I didn't have to come up with anymore plans to heal myself. I was able to go to God as I was. I could simply surrender everything to him.

At that moment, I committed to giving my brokenness to God- for real. I placed every single piece into his hands (yes, even those with sharp edges). **He showed me that my broken pieces in his hands were not jagged, but smooth. They didn't cut him because he created them. They had been thorns for me, but they were tools for him.** He showed me that I was just a masterpiece in progress.

One thing I love about God is that our broken pieces don't intimidate him; they don't invalidate his love for us. He is the Master potter; He's accustomed to making beauty from ashes. He has been waiting patiently for you to surrender your broken pieces to him, just like I did.

Leaders are not exempt from surrendering to God. If anything, we must be more attached to surrender than we ask our congregants to be. You have to ignore any guilt, embarrassment and shame attached to your broken pieces. You have to get past the pain that others may have caused you or pain you may have created yourself. **God won't force you to surrender, your surrender is an act of your will.**

Leaders must understand the importance and urgency with which we need to surrender our brokenness to God. Our lives depend on it, and so do the lives of those God has entrusted us to lead. If you won't surrender for yourself... Surender for them. The faster you hand God the broken pieces of your life, the faster he can remake, strengthen and fortify you. **<u>Your ability to lead is only as strong as your ability to surrender.</u>**

Prayer

*Thank you, Father, for allowing me to come to you in my brokenness. God, I am coming to you from an unfamiliar place, and frankly, it is **<u>not</u>** comfortable. I am accustomed to being strong and grounded, but now- I feel like a ship without a sail. However, I am willing to surrender myself to you -I relinquish all control and I submit to you the broken pieces of my life.*

God, take the broken pieces and put me back on the potter's wheel. Reshape my life as you see fit. I desire to be a vessel that can be used for your glory. God, I thank you in advance for crafting a newness in me. I am grateful that you provide your leaders with a safe place to come broken and leave better. Help me to always remember that I'm never too cracked, and my pieces are never too sharp to be placed in Your able hands.

REFLECT AND RESPOND

As leaders, it is often easy for us to help others find their way through healing processes, but difficult for us to navigate through our own journeys to self-better-ment. I believe this is largely due to the fact that we do not feel like we have safe places to hash out our inner feelings and reservations.

Most of our fragile moments are at the feet of God, in our secret places or in the shower. We're often trying to find inconspicuous places where we can be broken without judgement.

In Chapter 2, we discussed the necessity to surrender our brokenness. Whether your safe place of choice is God, a friend/family or a therapist, the fact remains that we all need somewhere to work through our issues as leaders.

Do you find it easy or difficult to surrender broken emotions to someone else for help? What are some of the obstacles you are faced with as you surrender your brokenness? Do you think you handle surrendering brokenness well? Does surrendering make you feel vulnerable? If so, how do you handle those feelings?

Take your time. Be detailed and specific.

_____

_____

_____

_____

_____

_____

_____

_____

_____

_____

_____

_____

_____

_____

_____

_____

DR. DEMETRA M. WILLIAMS

_____

_____

_____

_____

_____

_____

_____

_____

_____

_____

_____

_____

_____

_____

DR. DEMETRA M. WILLIAMS

WATCH YOUR TICKER

"Keep thy heart with all diligence; for out of it are the issues of life."
(Psalm 4:23)

Whatever is in your heart will come out. A large majority of leaders have mastered disguising their hearts. Many leaders' hearts are fortified behind massive walls of mistrust and feelings. **We don't trust a lot of people because we cannot afford to.**

In seasons of brokenness, a protected heart is a safe one. The devil attacks from every possible direction when brokenness creeps in, and an unprotected heart makes vulnerable leaders sitting ducks.

When I recognized this nakedness during my season of brokenness, I was intentional about saying less and reading more. My communion with God increased. I kept a scripture in my head and a song in my heart.

The most effective way to guard your heart is by fasting. Your fast does not necessarily have to be from food. I encourage you to evaluate anything in your life that sends subliminal messages to your heart. Whatever you discover, fast from it.

Turn off your phone, temporarily deactivate your social media accounts, and unplug the TV. Make a statement to your human nature and to the enemy that you only want God's messages in your heart.

It is vital to silence the aforementioned mediums because the things you hear and see can never be unheard and unseen. A large portion of what we let into our 'gates' via social media is contaminated.

Unfortunately, leaders are held to a different standard by society. Imperfect humans expect us to be perfect in all aspects of life. All it takes is one slip up; one lapse of judgment and social media makes our mistakes viral in a matter of minutes.

Leaders be cautious about what *you* are feeding into your soul. Although many rejoice to see leaders fall, we as leaders should not rejoice when others fall. At the same time, don't be harder on yourself than necessary when *you* fall. **Many leaders are their own worst critics. Give yourself the grace to grow; growth begins with the seeds that are planted in the soil of your heart.**

Beware! **Anytime you commit to clearing your heart from clutter and freeing your mind from distraction, the adversary will cloak himself in apparent calamity.** Your phone calls will increase, someone will inbox you and say that the things you post on social media are a great encouragement and petition you to 'keep them coming'.

The devil is extremely clever. **He keeps many leaders from taking time to self-heal because he's always sending distractions that tug on their gifts.** Most leaders say "I cannot afford to take a break" ... but truthfully, anyone who says that is relying on their strength to lead, and not God's.

God has charged us to be watchmen over the destinies of other people, but our watch is only as effective as our eyes are. Our leadership does not save people, it is the Light behind it that does the saving work. Don't be a leader that pours out until he/she is burnt out. Burnt out leaders give burnt out counsel.

Designate time solely for yourself. As a full-time wife, mother and educator, usually sleepy time for my household meant 'D-time' for me.

If I needed moments during the day, I'd steal away to the beach while my son was at school and my husband was at work. I would grab my favorite foods, find a cozy spot and let the wind beat against my face as the crash of the waves ministered to my heart.

Something about the solemnity of the Florida beaches allows tears to flow freely. This was my safe place to cry. I always felt as though I couldn't show emotion anywhere else because I was a leader... crying was a weakness and not a release.

I was accustomed to bottling up issues and locking them away. At the beach, there was a still quietness that allowed me space to meditate without over-thinking.

You need to find *that type* of space for yourself. Perhaps it's in a coffee shop, a secluded room in your house, a park in your neighborhood or even your car.

Find a safe place to go and let it out. Unclog your heart.

Be diligent on what you let go in or out of your heart. Know that you are a winner, and you were hand-selected to lead...

... So, *watch your ticker*.

Prayer

God, thank you for handpicking me to lead. Create in me a clean heart and renew a right spirit within me. I know it is a tall order, God, but I want to love like you- please give me a heart like Jesus.

Counsel me regarding my self-health. Advise me in mental and emotional wellness. Tell me when I need to take a "me" day.

As I navigate guarding my heart, cloak my tongue in wisdom to respond to those I lead without shunning or hurting them. Allow me time, grace and space to receive the maintenance I need on my heart.

REFLECT AND RESPOND

As leaders, we give a great deal of our heart to others on a daily basis. Sometimes our heart comes out in our instructions, other times- in our requests and vision for our organizations and teams.

The heart of the leader is what drives and gives momentum to movements and ministries. If our hearts become weary and worn, out by the day to day woes of leadership, those entrusted to our governance will surely suffer.

In Chapter 3, we discussed the importance of guarding and watching our hearts.

What are some things you've left your heart unprotected from in the past? How many of the heart wounds you've sustained over the years still hurt and affect you today? Do you have a therapist? Do you

*think that having an emotionally safe place is impor-
tant for you as a leader? Why or why not?*

Take your time. Be detailed and specific.

DR. DEMETRA M. WILLIAMS

DR. DEMETRA M. WILLIAMS

_____

_____

_____

_____

_____

_____

_____

_____

_____

_____

_____

_____

_____

_____

_____

_____

_____

_____

_____

_____

_____

_____

_____

_____

_____

_____

_____

_____

_____

_____

_____

DR. DEMETRA M. WILLIAMS

_____

_____

_____

_____

_____

_____

_____

_____

_____

_____

_____

_____

_____

_____

_____

_____

THE STRATEGY OF STILLNESS

"Be still, and know that I am God."
(Psalm 46:10)

"Y*ou gotta keep moving...*"

... That's what I told myself when facing adversity. I felt like being idle and still was a recipe for disaster. As a leader, it was tough for me to sit still because there was *always* something to be done.

To me, sitting still is a *chore*. I feel guilty when I'm not moving. I like to keep the ball rolling and the baton moving. I never want to waste time.

Refusal to be still is detrimental to the healing process of brokenness. Have you ever tried to move a broken item and noticed that because of its fragility, pieces fell off and got lost in the moving process?

Now imagine that you're that broken item. The more you attempt to move yourself while you're fragmented, the more pieces of yourself you leave behind.

Resist the urge to neglect yourself. Don't negate your emotional well-being for the sake of your spouse's or your family's. In the long run, placing the feelings of others over the health of your own emotions causes resentment and regret.

Pastors and church leaders, do not overload your plate. When you're exhausted, stop. By now, you've learned to recognize fatigue that's you-driven and not God-allowed. **If God isn't saying 'go', don't go.**

Leaders **must** master the art of stillness. We pour *out* more often than we are poured *into*. We lead and leave church exhausted- both physically and spiritually.

Our homes are often extensions of our churches; we leave the church, but the work follows us to our residential addresses. The plans we had to relax and wind down are often nullified by impromptu visits to hospitals, homes of members or emergency mediation sessions.

Don't feel bad when you cannot immediately meet the needs of your constituents; you're their leader, not their Savior.

If you're in full-time ministry *and* full-time workforce, maintaining balance is even more essential. Don't get bogged down with extra assignments and tasks as you try to climb the corporate ladder.

In your circle of friends, know when the take the pastoral hat off. Sometimes, we 'shepherd' our friends when they really just need a confidant.

Ask God for wisdom to navigate your daily life without neglecting your Divine duties.

I know you think busyness is helping you, but in reality, it is hurting you.

Imagine this.

You're sitting in 5pm traffic. You've got your music playing, windows down, a slight breeze hits your face as you watch the sunset awaiting a green light.

Ding.

Your check engine light comes on.

"Note to self: take car to mechanic this weekend. This weekend? Today is Tuesday... oh well, it'll just have to wait."

On Wednesday, a church member calls and asks if you can give words of inspiration at a funeral for her cousin's young son killed by gun violence. The family doesn't need the services to be held at your church, but all the other pastors they called are too busy to speak at the funeral.

Your wheels start turning, *"I can't allow this boy to be buried... I can't leave all those young people at a church-ripe for salvation- and not have a preacher to appeal to them. It won't take long, I'll go."*

Without asking God, you agree. *Your gift was tugging at you, it had to be God, right?*

By the time you get your car to the mechanic, more than a week has passed. You spent all of Saturday meeting and greeting grieving families, Sundays are slammed with church responsibilities and Mondays are your busiest days at work.

Your mechanic inspects your car and tells you he's got to keep it overnight to properly fix every issue. *Overnight?!? Nah, I can't do that. My son has basketball tomorrow and right after that is Bible Study.*

Instead of allowing the mechanic to fix the car, you tell him, *"I'll just come back when I have time to leave it here that long."* Against his counsel, you leave.

To make matters worse, the 'time' to leave the car with the mechanic never came, so you continued to drive around in a car that needed repairs. Because the car was functioning, it didn't matter to you that it needed maintenance.

Finally, three months later as you're pulling out of the car wash- your car breaks down. Shiny wheels, Febreze on the seats, *blown engine and head gasket. It looks great but needs a tow truck to get back home.*

This is how we are. We are vehicles that require repairs. We allow the fact that we are functioning to deter us from checking why the engine light came on in the first place.

We make appointments with our mechanic - God- and we never show up; or worse, we show up and place time limits on major repairs. We ignore what he says during the consultation and we take our barely functioning two-ton machines back to the road.

Just like our car began with a minor issue that evolved into a major one due to neglect, we become inoperable. We think that washing our exterior is more important than maintaining what's inside of the metal frame. **Eventually, instead of a few minor repairs- the entire vehicle needs to be redone.**

When we refuse to allot God time to perform routine maintenance on us, we are opening the door for a complete breakdown.

Learn the power of stillness; embrace the freedom to say 'No'.

Being still is an art, a craft; it is a skill every leader needs. Stillness enables God to work on us and gives him more opportunities to speak with us.

It is time for you to find your place of tranquility. As I mentioned before, that place looks different for everyone. The place you choose doesn't matter. What's important is your diligence in dedicating moments to be still.

Stillness is a strategy. It is your most effective weapon of warfare. Stillness allows you to hear the enemy because his steps aren't masked in the sound of your own and because your stillness allows you to have clearer communication with your Commander-In-Chief.

Prayer

God, I thank you because you are the master mechanic. You know what needs maintenance in my life before my check engine light comes on.

Please give me a heart to listen to your counsel. Don't let me operate a car that is one turn from breaking down.

Lord, I am grateful for the privilege to sit still and hear from you. Never allow me to feel guilty for dedicating time for self-maintenance. When my car needs a tune up, I want to bring it to you right away, with no delay.

Help me with the upkeep of this vehicle!

REFLECT AND RESPOND

As leaders, we often quickly become busy with life, and the hustle and bustle of our itineraries. Our lives are planned out weeks and months in advance. Many of us feel like we're in 100 places at once!

In Chapter 4, we discussed having a strategy of stillness. Leaders must be intentional about being still. Occasionally, we have to be willing to clear our schedules, not take any calls, and just...breathe.

Do you designate "still time" intentionally? How often? Do you think that the time you designate is appropriate recuperation time for the degree of involvement your leadership role demands? What do you do in your times of stillness? Do you truly think stillness is a strategy that leaders should employ? Why or why not?

Take your time. Be detailed and specific.

_____

_____

_____

_____

_____

_____

_____

_____

_____

_____

_____

_____

_____

_____

_____

DR. DEMETRA M. WILLIAMS

_____

_____

_____

_____

_____

_____

_____

_____

_____

_____

_____

_____

_____

_____

_____

_____

_____

_____

_____

_____

_____

_____

_____

_____

_____

_____

_____

_____

_____

_____

_____

_____

_____

_____

_____

_____

_____

_____

_____

_____

_____

_____

_____

_____

DR. DEMETRA M. WILLIAMS

_____

_____

_____

_____

_____

_____

_____

_____

RECEIVING RESTORATION

"And he said unto him, Arise, go thy way: thy faith hath made thee whole."
(Luke 17:19)

One of the most profound questions in Biblical history is *"Do you want to be made whole?"* When Jesus interrogated the man at the pool of Bethesda, I could not understand why.

"Are you serious? This guy has been sitting in this place for years, hoping someone would come along and rescue him. Yes, Jesus. Yes, he wants to be made whole!"

The truth of the matter is, Jesus asked the man that particular question because he saw past the man's desperation of speech and into his heart. **While this man was standing right before Jesus saying one thing, his history revealed another.**

This man was looking for the easy way out. He wanted *others* to take him to be healed and restored. He told Jesus that there was no one to take him to the water when the healing came down.

Most of us who read that story never stop and think, *"How did he get to the pool in the first place? Why didn't he drag himself into the pool after all this time?"*

The revelation of that question hit me hard many years after I read that story. There are people in life who are in places of despair, pain, hurt, heartache, guilt, shame, bitterness and brokenness who do **not** want to be made whole.

Some people are accustomed to trauma. When their lives aren't in trauma, they are lost. They're accustomed to living life in a negative space, and often like to wallow in it.

These are the type of people who live and hide behind "woe is me" stories; **they solicit helping seeking attention and sympathy, not solutions.**

If you don't know a person like that, chances are, you *are* that person. Don't be alarmed. This is a judgment-free zone. Sometimes we adopt the victim mentality unaware. The stress and bustle of life can cause great shifts in our persona that we don't recognize until someone hands us a mirror. **Sometimes even leaders experience temporary loses of focus.**

Leader, your peace can only be fully reinstated when you allow yourself to receive full restoration from God. I understand that as the responsible party for the destinies of countless others, it is sometimes difficult to shut your brain off; many leaders are over-thinkers.

Leadership requires continually putting out fires and coming up with on the spot renovations for the lives, hearts and minds of those you lead. This is why the adversary attacks the minds of leaders before he attacks anything else; this is why God begins the restoration process in the mind before he touches anything else.

He starts by restoring your earthly peace with a Kingdom one. God's version of peace is like a Hemi in a truck- an engine, only better.

His peace produces measurable results. You'll become a better problem solver and you'll have a calmer demeanor; you won't be easily angered or annoyed. You can smile and know that it was nobody but God that gave you *that* peace.

God's peace puts 'pep in your step'. You refuse to stay knocked down for long, your lenses become optimistic rather than pessimistic.

You walk through the fires of life like you're fire-proof, a confidence eerily resemblant of the three Hebrew boys (Daniel 3) who relied on God even in the face of persecution.

Please do not misconstrue the message of this chapter. Receiving restoration **does not** mean you become immune to trouble; **what it means is that your mind and your life become governed by a God-awareness instead of a trouble-awareness.**

Peace allows you to re-center and re-focus. Your speech will be renewed. The places you frequent will change. Most of all, others will notice the difference.

There's a catch.

You have to want it. Faith that God _can_ means nothing if you don't have the _will_ to allow him to work.

Once Jesus told a leper that his faith made him whole, but that faith was attached to action. Likewise, we have to have faith that God can do it and we have to be willing to take actions that match the level of faith we have.

Prayer

God, thank you for a renewed mind. Thank you for making me whole. Please grant me the strength, knowledge and wisdom to deal with the adversity that life brings.

Give me a winner's mentality. Remind me that I am victorious, and I can do all things through you. Take away any thoughts of defeat and victimization.

Change my mind; please don't allow me to wallow in my former state of brokenness.

Give me the courage to say, "Yes," I want to be made whole and the wisdom to accept it when you make me whole. Let me walk in victory because, in God, I know I am more than a conqueror.

Thank you for doing it for me. God, I surrender it all to you and trust that you will make me whole into a new masterpiece. So, I thank you in this masterpiece that is still a work in progress.

REFLECT AND RESPOND

As leaders, we spend a great deal of our time restoring others. We restore minds, hearts, order, and the like. People come to us in pieces and we put them back together or we direct them to someone who can; we orchestrate and oversee their healing processes.

In Chapter 5, we discussed receiving restoration. Givers of restoration can only give from the measure they've received. When two of the apostles encountered a man aside the road, they told him, "We don't have any silver, but what we do have, we will give you"— and proceeded to give the man the Spirit of God, in the gift of Jesus Christ.

Do you feel you deserve restoration? Have you put up a fight when God has asked your permission to heal and restore parts of you? If so, what caused you to resist? Do you think that unrestored leaders have an accurate view of the restoration process? Why or why not?

Take your time. Be detailed and specific.

_____

_____

_____

_____

_____

_____

_____

_____

_____

_____

_____

_____

_____

_____

_____

_____

_____

_____

_____

_____

_____

_____

_____

DR. DEMETRA M. WILLIAMS

NO LONELY I'S

*"Teaching them to observe all things whatsoever I
have commanded you:
and, lo, I am with you always, even unto the end of the
world. Amen."*
(Matthew 28:20)

W hen things aren't going right in my life, I retreat.

During my season of brokenness- amid my fragility and pain- I didn't want to be exposed. I isolated myself thinking it was the best thing for me; but isolation was a nail in the coffin.

Satan loves when we isolate ourselves. He wants us to create an island escape where we sit and muddle over our regrets, our deepest fears and insecurities.

We think these islands are sources of protection, but they actually make us more susceptible to the enemy's attacks. **These islands are where loneliness gets loud, where negativity has no limits, where helplessness is our pillow and worthlessness our bedspread.**

Isolation makes us feel like no one else shares our story, like it's us against the world. That's not true.

I *battled* because I didn't let people get close, but once I began to open up to other leaders, I found out that *I was not alone.*

Leadership roles put us in front of people, 24-7. **People are constantly looking for us to lead; they aren't looking for our struggle, they are looking for our instructions.**

I understand that some of you are hurting but can't show it. Others of you feel overlooked and forgotten, but you still manage to carry on. Many of you don't know *how* to lead and not *look* vulnerable.

Ask God to illuminate trustworthy leaders within your arena that you can be transparent with. You'd be amazed to hear how many of your peers share your experience(s).

Put your pride aside and be transparent. Leaders are real people who bleed. We love, hurt, laugh and cry. We have good days and bad days.

Remember that your calling to lead came from a God who knew all of that about you beforehand. That didn't deter his choice.

Once you can be real with yourself, you can be real with others. Share your testimony with others- it could save them... it could save *you*.

Say this aloud, *"I can share that I am **not** perfect. It is okay that I make mistakes. If it were not for God's grace, I don't know where I would be. Nevertheless, because of God's grace, I am still able to lead with every issue and flaw that I have!"*

Prayer

*God, I thank you for who you are. Thank you for letting me know that I am **not** alone, and others share my story.*

Thank you for providing me help for every trouble I've ever encountered. Please grant me the courage to share it.

Lord, I give you all of me- yes, the good and the bad. Thank you for never giving up on me.

*Because of You, God, I know I am **not** alone.*

Read and Reflect

As leaders, we find ourselves alone frequently. No matter how many people we surround ourselves with, we all have moments where we feel physically, mentally or spiritually alone.

The standard set by the organizations we represent, self-imposed standards and community expectations usually ostracize and single leaders out. In Chapter 6, we discussed the idea of loneliness and the ever-available presence of help in seemingly isolated situations.

How often do you feel like you're alone? Do you feel like feelings of loneliness are indicators of unhealthy thought patterns? Who are some of the people, if any- that have been placed in your life to provide you with confidants in your journey through life? Name them and take a moment to write out what they do for you personally (and spiritually, if applicable). When you're finished, call or text that person and express your gratitude for their companionship. You are not alone.

Take your time. Be detailed and specific.

_____

_____

_____

_____

_____

_____

_____

_____

_____

_____

_____

_____

_____

_____

_____

_____

_____

_____

_____

_____

_____

_____

_____

_____

_____

_____

_____

_____

_____

_____

_____

_____

_____

_____

_____

_____

_____

_____

_____

_____

_____

DR. DEMETRA M. WILLIAMS

_____

_____

_____

_____

_____

_____

_____

_____

_____

_____

_____

_____

_____

THE FOUR-LETTER WORD

"Ask, and it shall be given you; seek, and ye shall find; knock, and it shall be opened unto you" (Matt. 7:7)

H-E-L-P. Somebody. Anybody. Please. HELP ME.

If you are anything like me, asking for help is an arduous task. I am the type of person that loves to help others and will often be one of the first to offer assistance if I see someone in need. Ironically though, I am one of the last ones to ask for help.

I used to think of asking for help as a sign of weakness... a precursor of failure. I hated admitting I couldn't do something on my own.

In addition to those reservations, I also strongly felt that so many people that say they are willing to help are actually just providing a lip service.

During my time of need, the same people that shared that they would be there were *nowhere to be found*. When I humbled myself and asked for help, the people that I reached out to found every excuse and reason that they could not or would not help.

After facing that type of rejection, I felt like **I only had *me***. I wouldn't open myself up to be let down because it had happened so many times before. I refused to let it happen again.

The second reason I found it hard to ask for help was the way others' good deeds became town news. When someone was able to help me, they decided to tell others how they helped me. Not only did they tell others, but they also made me feel like a slave-like I was forever indebted to them because of their help.

It is not a great feeling when someone brings up how you were in need, and *"they helped you that one time"*. It is also disheartening to hear others come back and tell you how the help you received was shared with them by someone that you trusted.

We have to learn how to sow seeds and help people in secret. If you need to broadcast all of your good deeds, people won't solicit your assistance ever again. Are you like me? Are you like people? Either way, self-reflection at the place of help is needed.

As I reflected on my life, I reexamined my circle of influence. **I realized that some people needed to go, and some people need to be added to my circle.** I started to see a shift in certain relationships. I found myself opening up more to certain people. It was amazing because those were some of the people that I knew the shortest amount of time. Those people began to help me in ways that I never imagined.

The Bible tells us that all of our help comes from the Lord. The more I opened up, the more I started to see how God would use people to bless me. He began to work on me as I learned how to trust all over again. Most importantly, I was able to see how the new people in my circle were willing to help.

There was someone in my circle that would help by sending me encouraging words. At random times I would get a text message that simply said, *"I love you sis"* or *"You got this"* and *"I see you, girl."* That person did not know, but at that moment, I was down about being broken, and those messages would brighten my day. They gave me the courage to keep going.

I also found that there were people who were in my circle that would hold me accountable. Before I started writing this book, I shared what was placed on my heart about it with my God sister. One day, she called me and simply asked, *"Did you finish your book yet?"*

I was ashamed to say, *"No."* I didn't know what she would say next. Her reply stunned me. It was two words, *"It's needed."* That two-minute conversation encouraged me to finish a book that I had started a long ago. My God sister doesn't realize how meaningful that conversation was to this process. I didn't even realize that I needed those words, but I did. (Thanks, sis!)

God also sent someone who recognized through my tough exterior that my interior was fragile and broken. One particular time, she took me to lunch. When she initially asked how I was doing, I lied. She saw right through it. She wasn't buying it.

Knowing she didn't fall for my facade, I looked her in the eyes said: *"I am broken."* Tears rolled down my face as I began to share and open up to her. She was one of the first people that I had actually let in, and it felt *good.* I didn't fully understand how important it was to acknowledge my brokenness and then *deal with it.*

After I shared, sis grabbed my hand and began to pray. It was the type of prayer that touches you deep down in your soul- one that gives you hope and confidence- one that says, *"You're going to be okay."*

After the prayer, she looked at me and said: *"You are going to be alright now; let's eat a biiiig lunch -on me."* To know I had a sister girl that was willing to help me meant a lot to me.

Jesus allowed others to help him. When he fed the 5000 people, he needed the help of a young boy who had two fish and five loaves of bread in his lunch pail. When he rode into Jerusalem, it was on a donkey that belonged to someone else.

From the day of his birth to the time of his burial, the story of Jesus demonstrates his need for and acceptance of help from others.

Accepting help allows us to build relationships. Accepting help allows leaders to be more transparent with those we serve and those who serve us, but accepting help means dying to pride.

We have to swallow our pride and get rid of the notion that we don't need help or don't want to be a burden on someone. I've seen pride keep people from moving forward- pride has halted many leaders. **Some people think the most dangerous form of pride is arrogance, but pride that refuses help is really a tragedy.**

When dealing with being broken, it is crucial that you accept help. **The refusal to accept or ask for help will keep you in your brokenness much longer than you expect or want to be there.** If you're willing to relinquish your pride, God will send people that you can trust; people that genuinely want to be there for you.

As a leader, I attempted to handle everything on my own. If I assigned a task and a person was not doing it, I would do it myself. My pride wouldn't allow me to leave things be. I had to learn in leadership, you don't have to be the smartest person in the room, you just have to surround yourself with the smartest people.

Get a team that consists of people that are strong in areas that you are weak in. Learn how to use your resources and the people you have to get your assignments completed. Look at your circle of influence and make sure you are surrounded by people that love you and have your best interest at heart. **Allow others to help you.**

The relief you seek is coming from the Lord. Don't be ashamed to cry out to him for it and don't let foolish pride keep you from receiving it when it comes- **accept it and let it accelerate you.**

Prayer

God, I thank you for who you are. Please remove the prideful spirit in me that is afraid to ask for help. Show me those you have placed in my life to help me.

God, I ask that you give me a willingness to receive assistance in humility.

Thank you in advance for providing me with help, in this case, the help that is going to assist me in getting out of this broken point in my life.

Thank you for sending people to help me who love me and care about my success. God, I know this is a tough place, but in my brokenness, you have not left me or forsaken me. Thank you for your help.

Read and Reflect

As leaders, we rarely ask for help. Help is not for the hopeless; it is for those who have a healthy self-view. People who are unafraid to ask for help usually navigate leadership better than those who micromanage and attempt to be all things for all people.

In Chapter 7, we discussed the importance of asking for help.

Are you too proud to ask for help? If not now, have you ever been? Why or why not? What advice would you give a leader in need of extra hands to carry out their vision?

Consider this vignette:

Jermaine is a full-time graduate student and runs a farm for his grandfather on weekends. He also works at the university library with the work-study program. His grandfather has insisted for years that Johnny quit his work-study job and work on the farm full-time so he can make some "real money" and lighten his load so he can actually enjoy his studies. Jermaine is hesitant because he doesn't want to be stuck with his grandfather's farm post-graduation. He feels like his grandfather's solution is great for right now, but ties him up in the future. Advise Jermaine on how to accept (or decline) the help that has been extended to him.

Take your time. Be detailed and specific.

_____

_____

_____

_____

DR. DEMETRA M. WILLIAMS

DR. DEMETRA M. WILLIAMS

_____

_____

_____

_____

_____

_____

_____

_____

_____

_____

_____

_____

_____

_____

_____

_____

_____

_____

_____

_____

_____

_____

_____

_____

_____

_____

_____

_____

_____

_____

_____

DR. DEMETRA M. WILLIAMS

WILL TO BE CLAY

"Though he slay me, yet will I trust in him: but I will maintain mine own ways before him."
(Job 13:15)

Many leaders are hands-on. In our organization and/or ministries, very little action takes place without our knowledge or approval. Most of us are detail-oriented and prefer to have a good idea of the expected outcomes of projects and events.

In this way, we are similar to people who struggle with direction. They use GPS often and usually look at the instructions from beginning to end to get a good idea of the route they're taking. The more they know what to expect, the fewer surprises they figure they'll encounter along the way.

GPS gives us a sense of security on our journey. It allows us to take in the scenery and truly enjoy the ride we're on, rather than scramble at a missed turn, or follow an age-old paper map.

Giving God our broken pieces is similar to plugging a destination into a GPS. **His system- the Guaranteed Provision System is fool-proof**. We know the end we seek- healing. We know where we're beginning- brokenness. We have to learn to trust God to route and re-route us there; we have to overcome the nagging need to be in control of way we get to a place.

It is imperative that we trust God's process. We must become comfortable with the unknown. Not knowing when to turn left or right, when to go fast or slow, when to stop or keep going, or when you will get to your destination can seem daunting. Don't get discouraged. I want you to understand that God sees and knows all.

People who like to deviate from the GPS because "they know the roads" or "a better route" often end up at their destinations late and usually are turned around several times during the trip. By the time they get there, they're frustrated and worn out from the wear and tear of the extra time spent on the road.

Your healing journey cannot afford for you to get antsy and ignore the Guaranteed Provision System. If you stay the course, you're guaranteed to have provision for whatever you encounter along the way. You won't go without; you won't get worse and you won't get lost.

In a previous chapter, we introduced God as the Master Potter. It is important to know that the potter puts clay on the wheel in order to mold it into a new object. However, there are times during the process when things don't always turn out the way that they should. Instead of throwing away the broken pieces, the potter reuses the fractured parts as well. Not one piece is irrelevant. **All the broken pieces matter.**

God first starts by picking up our broken pieces. For us, this the first sign of relief. There's freedom in being relieved of the pressure and stress of putting yourself back together. Thanks to your surrender, that's God's job now.

After the clay is placed on the wheel, water is added. Adding water to the clay makes it more pliable; until the water is added, the clay is too hard to shape. **That is how many leaders are: too hard to shape and extremely reluctant to change.**

Throughout the scripture, the Word of God is illustrated as water. In the book of John, Jesus tells the Samaritan woman that there is living water that is everlasting. Just as the water makes the clay more pliable, so is the living water is necessary for change, shaping, and growth.

During your surrender, fueling yourself on the living water is vital. Make time to read the Bible. Sometimes what you read will overwhelm you, but don't be discouraged. Remember that you have a guide walking alongside you who will **not** allow anything to overtake you. If you don't know where to start, start with the story in John 4 about Jesus' encounter with the Samaritan woman and put yourself in her shoes.

After the water is added, the spinning of the wheel begins. This is used to start the molding and making of the clay. When God begins to spin our wheels, we sometimes feel like life is spinning out of control. For a person acclimated to being in control, this can be unsettling.

You may find yourself wanting to jump off the wheel but remember- trust the process. **If you get off prematurely, you may be in worse shape than you were placed on the wheel.** You're no longer firm, broken pieces; you're now soft, unshaped matter.

The spinning starts slow, but gradually gets faster. It is essential to know that no two molds of clay are identical, so each is handled differently by the potter. Crafting a pot is different from crafting a vase. They require different sharing speeds and velocities.

Likewise, you cannot compare how fast you are spinning to the speed of another piece of clay on the potter's wheel. This competitive spirit in the church has got to be dealt with. We cannot continue to compare our lives, victories and blessings to those of others. **We've been broken on different levels, so we're blessed on different levels.**

Next is the kneading process. During this phase, clay is stretched and molded into the piece the potter has in mind. While kneading, the potter gets rid of any air bubbles he detects.

The wrong people in our lives are like air bubbles, taking up unnecessary space. Negative thoughts and emotions are like air bubbles. Distractions are air bubbles. God has to remove these so that they don't affect his final product. Just like the bubbles find their way deep into the pliable clay, so are these things deeply embedded within us- and we often don't like to let go of them. We tend to hold on to these things tightly.

Loose your grip. These things need to go, don't be overcome by a spirit of complacency- don't allow them to stay any longer. You're not alone anymore. You no longer need any of those things to fill the void you put them in. You have to be willing to let it all go!

As the air bubbles are removed, the clay is ready to be kneaded firmly again. God will firmly knead you, and I hate to say it, but- it won't feel good. It's uncomfortable and will require a lot of reflection and sacrifice on your part.

You'll start to see what God is doing, but for some of you, it won't be a familiar picture. You're going to look different. Be confident that you're strong enough to endure the pain of being made firm again because God's hands are on you. He is taking his time to get you ready for the next step in the process... drying.

During the drying process, heat if often applied to the clay. This is where things really start to heat up in your life. You feel like you are going through the fire. You may lose friends, connections and acquaintances- even family. People you thought would always be in your corner won't be anywhere around.

Remember, heat is a purifier. God is using this time in your life to show you who is really down for you. **It will hurt, but it is necessary.**

The most challenging aspect of your surrender will be your capacity for patience. When potters are creating a new piece, they are not in a rush. They take their time working on the creation. Keep this in mind when you get frustrated with God's timing. **Although you are a leader, you're not the boss of God.** We grow so accustomed to having schedules and plans, that we become unnerved when we don't know or have control of the timetable.

We live in a culture of instant gratification. Cell phones have set a new normal for response times and communication. We've become extremely impatient and that has seeped over into many areas of our lives.

Think about the countless occasions when people have rushed into things; look how they turned out. When people rush into marriage, they miss critical characteristics- ones they would normally catch. In most of those cases, the marriages don't usually last long. When people rush and make hasty decisions, they overlook the fine print.

It is essential to allow God to take his time when he is molding you. He won't stop you from aborting the process, He'll just wait for you to come back around. Remember Jonah? He thought he could circumvent the process and he ended up spending some time in the belly of a fish- isolated from the world, surrounded by trash and whatever else was floating around in there. But eventually, where did he end up when he was spat out? Back where God wanted him.

When you allow God to reshape and remold you,

you invite him to give you upgrades. He has always wanted greater for you. Your broken pieces were instrumental in contributing to that greatness. As you reflect on this chapter, congratulate yourself on having the will to be clay on the wheel of the Potter.

Prayer

God, I thank you for choosing me – for hand-picking me as moldable clay. God, I thank you for another chance. Thank you for making me into something new.

Please give me strength to make it through the process; grant me grace so that I don't give up. Lord, I thank you in advance for making it through. I trust You!

Read and Reflect

As leaders, we help broken people find rejuvenation as "treasured jars of clay". Clay is one of the best examples we can give when addressing the human traversal through processes of change.

In Chapter 8, we discussed the vitality of one's willingness to be clay on the Potter's Wheel. Clay is rigid when it dries, but when wet, it is a pliable and easily moldable element.

Think of yourself as a type of clay. Are you rigid and unmovable? Or are you wet and pliable? Are you as coachable as you expect those you lead to be? Why or why not? Do you resist seasons of reshaping and remolding? Why or why not? If you resist or push back against change, do you think the reasoning is due to the trauma we discussed in Chapter 1? Why or why not?

Take your time. Be detailed and specific.

_____

_____

_____

_____

_____

_____

_____

DR. DEMETRA M. WILLIAMS

_____

_____

_____

_____

_____

_____

_____

_____

_____

_____

_____

_____

_____

_____

_____

_____

DR. DEMETRA M. WILLIAMS

MOURNING MEMORIES

"Weeping may endure for a night, but joy cometh in the morning."
(Psalm 30:5)

It's okay to cry. I don't know how many times I had to tell myself that. In my mind, crying was a habit of the weak- those who were unfit to lead. No matter what happened in my life, my pride would **not** let me *cry*.

When I had to deal with tough situations, I just went numb and busied myself with anything I could get my hands on. Numbing my mind and emotions to the change God was making inside of me was a coping mechanism. I was literally watching God take every piece that I surrendered to him and make me into someone *else*.

It didn't matter to me that this new me was God's true version, I was mourning the old me- the woman who died on the wheel. It hurt. The excitement of the new was not loud enough to drown out the screams for the old- the comfortable. Worst of all, I felt bad for feeling bad about changing...

...until one day... *"It's okay"*. It was as if God had been living inside my mind or eavesdropping on my conversations with myself. He gave me the strength to give myself permission to cry.

I dedicated a period of mourning for my old self. I eulogized my old life, my old philosophy, psychology and personality. I came to terms with this exodus into newness: the new me was a much better version of the old me. I had to grieve and get on with my life.

Mourning the old me wasn't as easy as you'd think. **Change requires pain. Pain is grievous.** I literally went through the five stages of grief as God changed me before my eyes.

Stage One: Denial

"I can't believe this is happening to me; I can't believe God trusts me enough to change me."

I didn't think I deserved to be made whole. *I wasn't worth it.* I was guilty and I couldn't let it go. I was holding on to the memories of things said and done (by myself and others). *Why would God waste time changing someone who so easily fell into a broken state? Had I not proven to him that I wasn't cut out for this?*

Stage Two: Anger

"Wait a minute, what did I do to deserve being broken like this? Why do I have to relinquish control of everything I know?"

I was angry because I had found an odd sense of comfort with the feeling of brokenness; I'd learned how to live with it.

Now I had to deal with a *new* feeling, and I didn't like it. I am a person who loves consistency. I'm rigid about schedules and itineraries; I do **not** like deviations.

"Everything around me is changing."

I was so upset that God was uprooting everything that I knew... and exposing it in the process.

Stage Three: Bargaining

"Can I at least keep this?"

I tried to bargain with God. I didn't want him to remove everything. After all, there were parts of me that were okay, and I wanted those parts to stay. If God was going to remake me, I figured I should have a say- you know- help him make the changes.

There were times that I found myself thinking I knew what was *best* for me. That leadership zeal was a big chip on my shoulder. *"God, I am a fixer. You made me to help fix others. Let me help you fix me, too."*

Like the man at the pool of Bethesda, I had made a mat and found a new home in brokenness. In order for God to get me up, he had to do an upheaval of the entire foundation, not bits and pieces.

Stage Four: Depression

"I'm worried about things all the time."

Depression is rooted in worrying. I hate to admit it, but there were times that I would sit at night and worry relentlessly. My mind never seemed to shut off. It began with me worrying about things I didn't do one day and progressed into me worrying about something I did or said *two or even ten years* ago.

I worried about what people would think or say when they found out that I didn't have everything together.

"They're going to judge me. They're going to think I don't have the skills or the fortitude to lead people."

"Wait, what about my marriage? Is it strong enough to continue when I'm changing? Am I worthy enough? I've done so much wrong. Will my husband like the new me?"

I worried about my son. *"Is this new mommy better than the old mommy he's grown to love?"*

Even worse, my refusal to address these worrisome thoughts at the door created a snowball effect that-without the grace of God- could have easily spiraled into depression.

Stage Five: Acceptance

"Ok God, I'm ready to listen- for real."

I had come to the point where I accepted what God allowed. God is sovereign, omnipotent and omnipresent. He longs to speak with us, but he won't force a conversation. Now that I was ready to listen wholeheartedly, he spoke:

"DeMetra, for so long, you've accepted mediocrity because it was getting the job done. I want to take you to a new level in every aspect of your life. You're looking at snapshots of you, I have the whole picture in my view."

Hearing those words from God gave me closure and peace about the brokenness and the death of the old me. I felt a difference in my mind; I could accept that things were *never* going to be the same.

As a leader, you **must** be willing to give God *total control* of the molding process without trying to "help". Allow yourself to go through the five stages of grief. *"Be confident of this, that he who began a good work in you will carry it on to completion"* (*Philippians 1:6, NIV*).

Prayer

God, thank you for never giving up on me. When I wanted to turn around and run back to the old me, you reminded me that that person is dead.

Lord, thank you for allowing me time to grieve the old me while you continued to work on the new me. Thank you for showing me that it is okay to cry, and the release of the old is needed.

Thank you for taking me through the grieving process; for holding my hand as I made it through every step and never leaving me alone.

Lord, although this process is stringent, I still trust you. You are awesome and worthy of praise.

REFLECT AND RESPOND

As leaders, pastors deal with death frequently. They eulogize many and oversee/officiate countless funerals. Young, old, rich, poor; everyone has a departure date.

In Chapter 9, we discussed mourning memories. Just like we grieve and mourn our loved ones who transition from earth to afterlife, so must we mourn and grieve the old versions of us who die during our seasons of pruning and changing.

What are some things about the old you that you miss? Be honest. Do you now see that although those parts weren't bad, they were still detrimental to your purpose and destiny on earth? Do you struggle with memories of the "you" that you had to give up? What mental re-routes can you put in place to make sure you have a healthy grieving relationship with the "you" of the past?

Take your time. Be detailed and specific.

_____

_____

_____

_____

_____

_____

_____

_____

_____

_____

_____

_____

_____

_____

_____

DR. DEMETRA M. WILLIAMS

_____

_____

_____

_____

_____

_____

_____

_____

_____

_____

_____

_____

_____

_____

_____

_____

NEW IS GOOD NEWS

Rejoice in the Lord always: and again I say, Rejoice."
(Philippians 4:4)

Celebrations are appropriate.

Celebrations are in order.

There's never *nothing* to celebrate. The fact that God took your broken pieces and made them into a masterpiece *deserves celebration*.

When things got tough, you did not give up. When the process got rough, you didn't throw in the towel. You trusted the process, you stayed in the race.

Most leaders would rather be the cheerleader than the celebrated. Many of us would rather push someone else in the spotlight than to be in it ourselves. However, being celebrated maintains balance in your psyche.

Although you feel like nothing you do deserves celebration, God sees things differently. This is why he rewards patience, perseverance and obedience. He knows that overcoming human nature is difficult and that our wills are strong. **At any time, we could choose not to serve him, but we don't.**

It's tough to be happy or celebrate when you only focus on the negative things in your life or about your character. You will never feel worthy of celebration if you're zeroed in on guilt, shame, heartache and pain.

After identifying my brokenness, I *celebrated* the first step of a new journey. I know some may look at it as silly, but I knew that after the recognition *change* would follow. **I celebrated that I trusted God enough to give him my broken pieces.**

I *celebrated* because I knew I was on the right path; I knew each step would take me closer to God and closer to being a new masterpiece.

We often look at addicts and wonder *why* people celebrate the fact that they go to rehab. Those that have dealt with addiction understand that admitting the problem and seeking help is a big deal! They know that the hardest part of the process is *taking the first step*.

That is what God wants for us. He wants us to take the first step.

It is important that we celebrate even the small milestones of life. We don't have to wait until something huge happens.

We hear so much about short term and long-term goals. Short term goals keep us encouraged as we strive to meet our long-term goals. **Be sure to celebrate every time you meet a short-term goal.**

Did you eat right or go to the gym today? *Celebrate* that! It doesn't matter if you are on day 1 or day 101, the fact that you made a decision to do better for your body is celebratory.

God commands us to rejoice. He doesn't say 'when things are good"- he says "always".

You must make rejoicing an intentional habit. I did this by committing to writing out everything I needed to get accomplished and marking things off as the day progressed.

It felt good to cross things off my list after I completed them. This plan worked for me, perhaps it will work for you, too.

Eventually, I began rewarding myself for completing tasks. If I finished over half my tasks before lunch, I would give myself a couple of extra minutes for lunch.

When I made it a point to celebrate the small things in life, it allowed me to be more open to celebrating the significant things. I learned that I didn't have to make myself smaller so others could feel bigger; there's enough room for us all to be big.

In light of all that God has brought you through, you deserve to be celebrated.

Even while reading this book, *I celebrate you* because you made a decision to *do* something. You did not just sit in your brokenness; you looked for a way out.

Cheers to you and your willingness to be made whole!

Prayer

God, thank you for YOU.

Thank you for allowing me to find reasons to rejoice again. Thank you for giving me something to celebrate.

Thank you for taking me from my brokenness to newness in you.

Now, give grace to continue this new journey. Thank you for allowing me to live, love and laugh again.

READ AND REFLECT

As leaders, we seldom discuss what's new with us. We leave accolades and celebrations to our

organizations and teams— and they usually manifest in once a year appreciation dinners or events.

In Chapter 10, we discussed the beauty of newness. Just as gardeners are excited about the first sprouts, just as constructors are excited about new tools- so must we be excited about the newness that follows extended periods of brokenness. Once a year is not nearly enough to celebrate the new in you.

Do you celebrate new things, mindsets and movements when they happen to you? Do you allow others to celebrate you? What are ways you can be more open to receiving well-deserved celebratory congratulations? If you've turned down the opportunity to be celebrated by your team, commit to apologizing to them. Accepting thanks and praise doesn't mean you're seeking attention, it means you're humble enough to allow those in your sphere of influence to celebrate a valuable resource- YOU- in their lives.

Take your time. Be detailed and specific.

_____

_____

_____

_____

_____

_____

_____

_____

_____

_____

_____

_____

_____

_____

_____

_____

_____

_____

_____

_____

_____

_____

_____

_____

_____

_____

_____

_____

_____

_____

_____

_____

_____

DR. DEMETRA M. WILLIAMS

_____

_____

_____

_____

_____

_____

_____

_____

_____

_____

_____

_____

_____

_____

_____

_____

OWN THE UPGRADE

"Therefore if any man be in Christ, he is a new creature:
old things are passed away; behold, all things are become new."
(*2 Corinthians 5:17*)

G od has taken you off the potter's wheel, and you have made it past the molding and kneading. You survived one of the toughest times of your life. Although it did not feel good, you never gave up; you've officially transformed from brokenness to wholeness.

The journey from brokenness to wholeness is like upgrading a computer or a cell phone. We purchase these devices, usually not accounting for the growth and changes we will go through over the years of owning them.

Most people do not purchase devices to last them for three years in terms of storage to capacity- they just want something that's reasonably priced and works for their life right now.

Many people who frequent tech stores for upgrades aren't there because they want to be, they're there because they have to be. People don't like to pay for upgrades upfront because the price for more storage and better performance is more expensive.

It's the same way with leadership. The most rewarding seats of leadership are the most uncomfortable and painful ones. They cost us time, money and friendship. They have a high price tag but yield high dividends and are stable and reliable connections to our destinies.

You're an upgrade now, own it.

In the same way that you don't upgrade a phone or computer just to re-upload the old, God didn't upgrade you for you to re-live your past. **Every**

experience we have in life equips us for our destinies but fills in gaps in the stories of others.

Leaders are gap-fillers. We show people how to come out of hopeless situations with victory; how to overcome the odds without losing humility. We are real-life images of show-n-tell. Our transparency allows people to see God's light and inspires them not to give up.

The more willing we are to own our upgrades, the more effective our testimonies become. No longer can you spend life staring at your rearview; there's an assignment near you that needs you focused on forward progress!

One of the hardest things about operating in your newness and owning your upgrade is letting go of the past. Let go of the people- their seasons are over. Your capacity is greater and linking up with older, slower devices will jack up your speed and functionality.

I know it's tough to forsake the familiar, but familiarity breeds contempt. When people see movement in your life, they often want to latch on and catch a ride. You're a leader, not a taxi. People can follow you, but they've got to travel with their own two feet.

Be free from the burden of carrying people and bags from your past. Carrying baggage slows you down and robs others of the advantage of having an encounter with Jesus through you.

Don't be selfish, the world deserves the new you.

The new you can tell your story. It is important to tell others *how* you made it. Your story is a beginning point for someone else's.

The new you can help someone else. Sharing how you didn't let your brokenness define your life can encourage others to not give up.

The new you can inspire.

God took your broken pieces and made YOU into a masterpiece...

... the fragmented pieces didn't turn him off. He didn't cast you aside—- he graced you to lead while you were broken.

Prayer

God, thank you for upgrading me. Upgrades are expensive but they are worth it. Thank you for seeing me as expensive and worthy when I viewed myself as cheap and valueless.

Help me to forget the negativity behind me and to press forward in newness.

*God, never allow me to forget that it was **you** who did this for me. Allow me to be confident but never arrogant.*

Most of all, remind me to take time out to celebrate being a new masterpiece. You graced me to lead while broken so that I can lead others out of brokenness and for that Lord, I give you all the glory.

READ AND REFLECT

As leaders, we are so busy helping others become the best versions of themselves that we don't stop and

appreciate our own personal progress. Just as we're unable to restore without first receiving restoration, the same is true of putting microscopes on change in others: we've got to use it first.

In Chapter 11, we discussed owning intrinsic upgrades.

What are some "upgrades" that have been added to your character/personality in the past month? Quarter? Year? 3 years? Have you taken the time out to stop, celebrate, and actually possess those personal achievements? If so, how? If not, make time to do so , and document how it felt to do so. Lastly, as we culminate this book, take time and give thanks to God, your safe places and anyone else who has played a role in your journey from brokenness to better. You're no longer leading while broken— and that, my friend, is a blessing.

_____

_____

_____

_____

_____

_____

_____

_____

_____

_____

_____

_____

_____

_____

_____

_____

_____

_____

_____

_____

_____

_____

_____

_____

_____

_____

_____

_____

_____

_____

_____

_____

_____

DR. DEMETRA M. WILLIAMS

_____

_____

_____

_____

_____

_____

_____

_____

_____

_____

_____

_____

_____

_____

_____

DR. DEMETRA M. WILLIAMS

ABOUT THE AUTHOR

Dr. DeMetra Williams was born in Long Beach, California, but spent most of her life in Ohio.

She has two bachelor's degrees in History and Secondary Education respectively (University of Cincinnati); a master's degree in Educational Leadership (Troy University), and a Doctor of Education in Educational Leadership (North Central University).

Dr. Williams has been in the field of education for the past 17 years and has a heart for young people.

As the wife of a Senior Pastor, Dr. Williams serves and works arduously with youth. She served a tenure of over 10 years in the COGIC IYD (specifically, with the Young Women of Excellence). After serving as a Chairlady for over a decade, Dr. Williams was appointed President of the Western Florida 2nd Jurisdiction Youth Department (Bishop Larry Perkins, Prelate).

At the national level of COGIC she serves the International AIM convention on the PR and Marketing team. She also serves on the Advisory Board for the National COGIC Youth Church.

In recognition of her service, Dr. Williams was recognized as one of the COGIC Achievers 20 under 40- a distinguished honor given to the top 20 members of the COGIC church under age 40 whose reach extends outside of their churches and into their communities and careers.

Of all the positions that she holds, her most important is being a wife and a mother. Dr. Williams currently resides in Apopka, Fl with her husband Jeffery Paul Williams II, and her son, Jeffery Paul Williams III (Trey).

Made in the USA
Columbia, SC
16 June 2023

17867251R00093